CRISTIANO RONALDO
THE ULTIMATE FAN BOOK

Copyright © Carlton Books 2014, 2016, 2017

First published in 2014 by Carlton Books Limited
20 Mortimer Street, London W1T 3JW

This edition published in 2017

A CIP catalogue record for this book is available from the British Library

10 9 8 7 6 5 4 3 2 1

ISBN 978-1-78097-920-5

Printed in Dubai

CRISTIANO RONALDO
THE ULTIMATE FAN BOOK

THIRD EDITION

Iain Spragg

CARLTON
BOOKS

CONTENTS

Right: Ronaldo led Portugal to glory in the 2016 UEFA European Championships and his vital contributions included the first penalty in the quarter-final shoot-out victory over Poland.

INTRODUCTION

From his early years on the Portuguese island of Madeira to becoming a superstar in Madrid, the story of Cristiano Ronaldo's career is an incredible footballing blockbuster.

Cristiano Ronaldo is the most famous footballer on the planet and thanks to his record-breaking performances in the red of Manchester United and the white of Real Madrid, he is now regarded as the game's greatest player.

The Portuguese magician is football's ultimate showman and no one can match the explosive entertainment he provides on the pitch. Watching Ronaldo is a masterclass in how to destroy the opposition – in style!

Worshipped by his millions of fans and feared by every team he plays against, Ronaldo has come a long way since he joined his first team in his hometown of Funchal as a young boy and began his journey to fame and fortune. It has been a remarkable rise and on the way he has lit up every pitch he has played on with his incredible skills.

The Real Madrid star has won every major club trophy in England and Spain, as well as the UEFA Champions League and FIFA Club World Cup – and he added to his incredible collection of winners' medals after leading Portugal to glory at Euro 2016.

He is his country's most capped player and top scorer of all time, a Spanish league record-breaker in front of goal and a three-time winner of the Ballon d'Or, the award given each year to the world's best player.

Cristiano Ronaldo: The Ultimate Fan Book is a celebration of the genius of the Portuguese striker and his amazing achievements. It takes you on a journey that starts in Madeira, passes through Lisbon and Manchester up to his arrival at Madrid's Bernabeu stadium, at which he has become the world's greatest player.

The book also looks at Ronaldo's life away from football, his family and his fame, as well as how hospital surgery helped him overcome a heart problem as a teenager.

You don't have to be a Manchester United or Real Madrid supporter to love Ronaldo's unique talents and this book is the ultimate guide to the ultimate player.

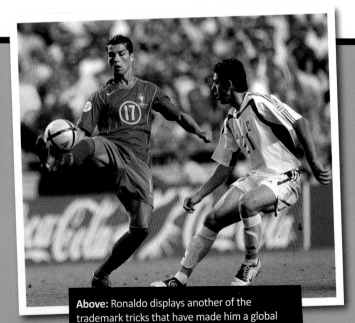

Above: Ronaldo displays another of the trademark tricks that have made him a global superstar.

Below: No-one has scored more international goals for Portugal than the Real Madrid hero.

Above: Ronaldo won his third UEFA Champions League final in 2016, his second and Real Madrid's 11th, and scored with the final attempt in the penalty shoot-out against Atletico Madrid.

THE EARLY YEARS

The Real Madrid star was an unruly pupil at school!
But away from the classroom it was obvious he had a
very special talent.

Ronaldo was born on February 5, 1985 on the Portuguese island of Madeira. He was christened Cristiano Ronaldo dos Santos Aveiro by his parents because his father, José, was a big fan of an old Hollywood actor called Ronald Reagan. When Ronaldo was born, Reagan had become President of the USA.

The family lived in the city of Funchal on the south coast of the island. José worked as a gardener for the local council while his mother Maria was a cook. They were not rich but the lack of money only helped to bring Ronaldo and his two older sisters, Elma and Liliana Cátia, and his big brother, Hugo, closer together.

Above: Nine-year-old Ronaldo's identity card for the 1994–95 season, when he played for Clube Futebol de Andorinha in Funchal, Madeira.

"I was brought up with nothing," Ronaldo said. "We were very poor. I had no toys and no Christmas presents. I shared a room with my brother and two sisters and my parents slept in the other. It was a small space but I didn't mind. I'm incredibly close to my brother and two sisters and we loved being together. For us it was normal, it was all we knew. Everybody around us lived the same way and we were happy."

When he was eight years old, Ronaldo joined the junior team at his local club, Andorinha. But while his first football coaches were amazed by his skills, his school teachers were not as impressed. "I was not thick but I was not interested in school," he said. "I was expelled after I threw a chair at the teacher. He disrespected me. When I got to 14 ... I thought I was maybe good enough at that time to play semi-professionally."

His family agreed with him and decided that he should concentrate on his football rather than his studies. Ronaldo was now on his way to becoming the world's greatest footballer.

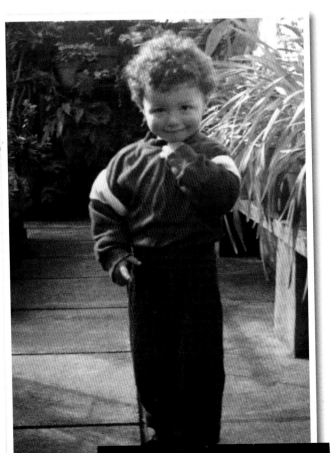

Above: Ronaldo grew up in a poor family but enjoyed a happy childhood on the Portuguese island of Madeira.

Below: Since signing for Real Madrid, Ronaldo has become the game's greatest player.

THE NEXT STEPS

The superstar began to make a big impression in his home country of Portugal, despite a frightening problem with his health.

Ronaldo spent two seasons with Andorinha but it was already obvious that the boy was a special talent. So in 1995 he switched clubs, joining Nacional, in his hometown of Funchal. He was still only 10 years old but this move had a big effect on his career.

In his first season at Nacional, Ronaldo's Under-11 team won their league title and word was beginning to spread about the team's skinny midfielder with the outrageous skills. "People knew I was a talented kid," Ronaldo said.

The talent spotters at big club Sporting Lisbon, based in Portugal's capital city, had heard of him and he was invited to the club for a three-day trial. It meant leaving the island of Madeira and heading to the Portuguese mainland but Ronaldo was determined to take his big chance. After the trial, Sporting Lisbon decided to offer him an apprenticeship.

Ronaldo continued to impress the coaching staff at Sporting, but at the age of 15 he was suddenly diagnosed with a serious heart problem and the club decided he needed an operation to cure it.

The problem was that his heart was beating too fast, even when he wasn't running. His mother Maria said, "The people in charge at Sporting called me and I went to Portugal where I had to sign some papers so he could be treated in hospital. I was worried because he might have to give up playing football. But the treatment went well and after a few days he was back training again."

Luckily, Ronaldo make a complete recovery and starred for Portugal at the European Under-17 Championship held in Denmark in 2002, starting in the group games against France and Ukraine. When he got back to his club, he was promoted to the reserves. So the teenager had almost made it to the first team and a few months later took the final step to become a full senior player.

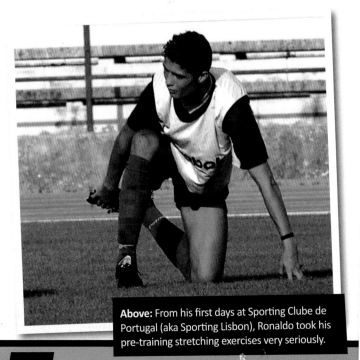

Above: From his first days at Sporting Clube de Portugal (aka Sporting Lisbon), Ronaldo took his pre-training stretching exercises very seriously.

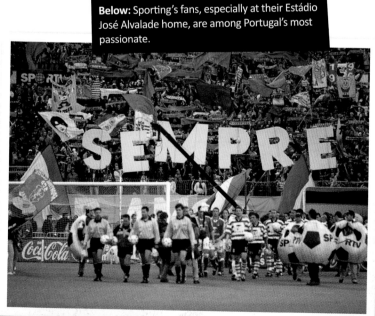

Below: Sporting's fans, especially at their Estádio José Alvalade home, are among Portugal's most passionate.

Above: Even in training, Ronaldo was all business because he knew that perfecting his technique would take him a long way.

HIS BIG BREAKTHROUGH

Just a few months after his 17th birthday, Ronaldo made the headlines with a sensational league debut for Sporting Lisbon.

Although everyone in Lisbon knew just how talented Ronaldo was, he was not yet well known outside the city. But all that changed in October 2002 when the teenager was given his senior debut for the club.

The Sporting manager, Laszlo Boloni, decided Ronaldo was ready to perform with all the top professionals and put him in the team to play against Moreirense in a Portuguese Primeira Liga game at the club's home ground, the Estádio José Alvalade.

The time had come for Ronaldo to show the world his magic and the 17-year-old did not disappoint. Sporting won the match – and Ronaldo scored twice!

His first goal came in the first half after he picked up the ball inside the Moreirense half and set off on an amazing run. His speed took him past one sliding tackle and when a second player closed in on him, he produced an outrageous stepover which left the embarrassed defender behind him. The Moreirense goalkeeper rushed out but Ronaldo did not panic and unleashed a deadly low shot which hit the back of the net.

His second goal came in second-half injury time. Sporting were awarded a free-kick near the corner flag and as the ball came sailing into the area, it was Ronaldo who jumped above the Moreirense defence to head home and seal the team's 3–0 victory.

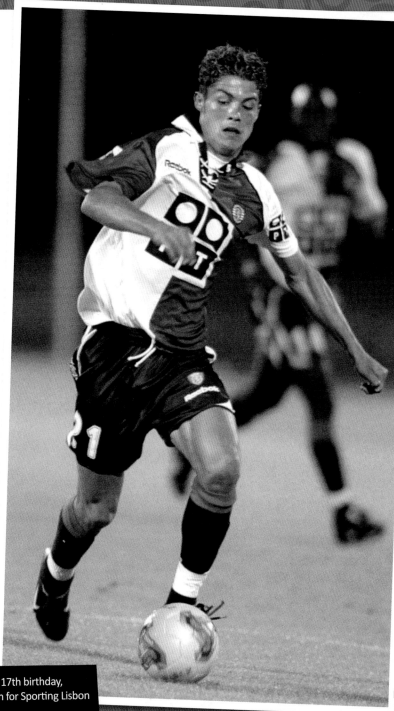

Above: Five months after his 17th birthday, Ronaldo saw first-team action for Sporting Lisbon in preseason friendlies.

A star had been born. Every football fan in Portugal had now heard of the youngster from Madeira and his life would never be the same again.

Ronaldo made 24 more Primeira Liga appearances for his club during the 2002–03 season as Sporting finished third in the table. He also scored twice in three Portuguese Cup games. He was suddenly the hottest property in Portuguese football and although he didn't yet realise it, it would not be long before one of the most biggest and famous clubs in the world was knocking on Sporting's door trying to sign the teenager.

Above: A month after his first-team debut for Sporting, Ronaldo was showing off his ball skills to Maritimo defenders Albertino (left) and Joel.

MOVING TO ENGLAND

After just one full season with Sporting, Ronaldo was on his way to Old Trafford to play for the mighty Manchester United.

It was not long after Ronaldo's amazing debut for Sporting that some of Europe's top clubs began to take notice of the teenager. Both Liverpool and Barcelona were interested and Ronaldo even met Arsenal manager Arsene Wenger at the club's training ground to discuss joining the Gunners.

The race for his signature was hotting up but there could only be one winner – Manchester United.

What really sealed the deal was a friendly between Sporting and United in the summer of 2003 in Lisbon. The game was staged to celebrate the opening of Sporting's new stadium and Ronaldo was the man of the match as his Portuguese team beat the Premier League champions 3–1.

Six days later United signed him for £12.24 million, handing the 18-year-old the number seven shirt worn by David Beckham the previous season. Manager Sir Alex Ferguson admitted it was Ronaldo's dazzling display in the friendly in Portugal that convinced him he was going to become a star.

"He is an extremely talented footballer, a two-footed attacker who can play anywhere up front," Ferguson said after the deal was done. "After we played Sporting last week the lads in the dressing room talked about him constantly and on the plane back from the game they urged me to sign him. That's how highly they rated him. He is one of the most exciting young players I've ever seen."

It was the start of a brilliant six seasons for Ronaldo in England in which he won eight major trophies, was voted the best player in Europe in 2008 and scored more than 100 goals for the Red Devils. Old Trafford worshipped their Portuguese playmaker and Ronaldo repeatedly repaid the fans with some of the most magical football they had ever seen.

Above: Ronaldo takes the ball away from Nicky Butt in summer 2003; within a week they were Manchester United team-mates.

Below: Ronaldo in UEFA Champions League action for Manchester United, taking on Porto's Maniche in 2003.

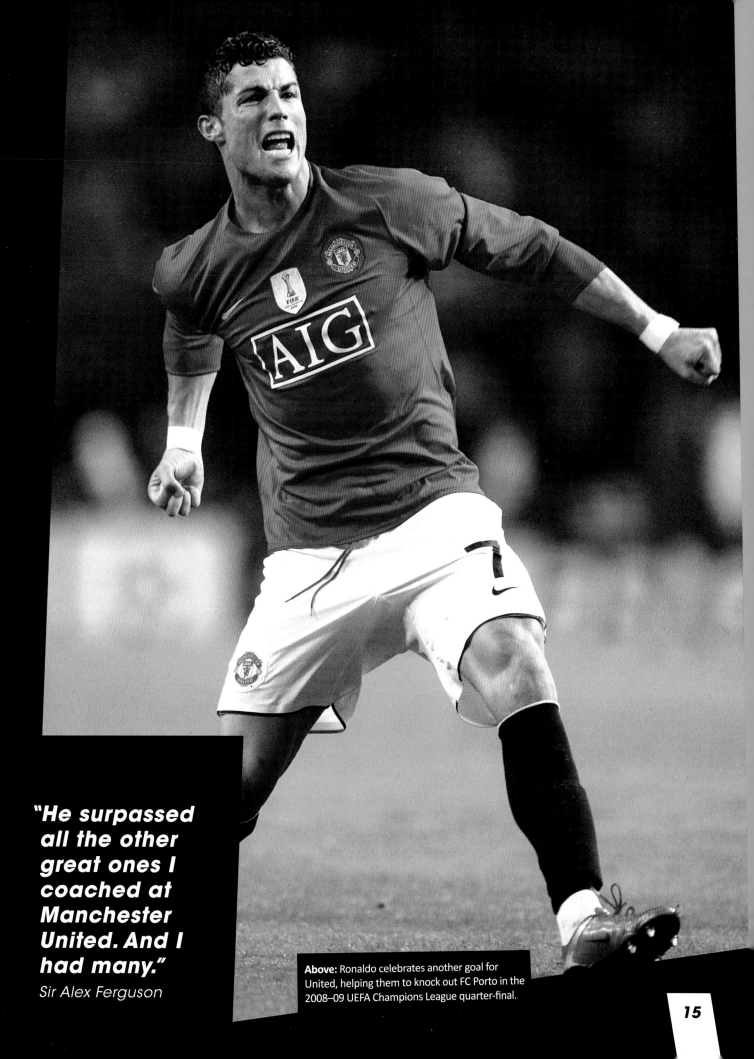

> *"He surpassed all the other great ones I coached at Manchester United. And I had many."*
>
> *Sir Alex Ferguson*

Above: Ronaldo celebrates another goal for United, helping them to knock out FC Porto in the 2008–09 UEFA Champions League quarter-final.

NEW NATIONAL HERO

Football is Portugal's number one sport and in Ronaldo the country has a special player to make the nation proud.

Before Ronaldo burst onto the scene more than 10 years ago, the two most famous names in the history of Portuguese football were two players called Eusebio and Luis Figo. Both were amazing flair players who won all the big trophies at club level and gave some incredible performances for the national team.

Ronaldo however has eclipsed them both and is now recognised as the greatest player Portugal has ever produced.

It all began when the then Sporting Lisbon star was given his international debut as a teenager in a friendly match against Kazakhstan in 2003. He played for just 45 minutes, but he was in the starting line-up for his second cap two months later when Portugal smashed Albania 5–3. It was already obvious Portugal had unearthed a new hero.

Above: Cristiano Ronaldo was just 18 when he won his first cap for Portugal against Kazakhstan in 2003.

His first full 90 minutes of action came during Euro 2004 and the dramatic penalty shootout win over England in Lisbon in the quarter-finals. Although Portugal were ambushed in the final by Greece, Ronaldo was now a firm fixture in the team.

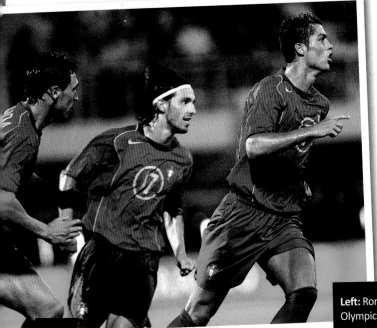

Left: Ronaldo was on target during the 2004 Olympic Games against Morocco.

Since then the striker has surpassed both Eusebio and Figo and rewritten the Portuguese record books.

By the end of the 2015–16 season, and Portugal's amazing victory in Euro 2016, Ronaldo had won 133 caps for his country. Figo had held the record with 127 appearances but Ronaldo passed that milestone when Portugal faced Austria in the second game of European Championship finals.

He also had netted a staggering 61 international goals, easily beating the previous Portuguese record of 47 set by former teammate Pauleta.

The international records set by the remarkable Ronaldo do not stop there. No one has played in more European Championship finals games (21) than Ronaldo or scored more goals in the finals (9). He is also the only player to score in four Euro finals tournaments (2004, 2008, 2012 and 2016).

It's an awesome list of achievements from Portugal's greatest ever footballer and, with time still on his side, he has the chance to smash even more records.

Below: Ronaldo's goal for Portugal against Wales in the Euro 2016 semi-final in Lyon was the 61st of his record-breaking international career.

WORLD CUP STAR

Having played in three World Cups – in Germany in 2006, South Africa in 2010 and Brazil in 2014 – Ronaldo is one of international football's biggest stars.

It is every player's dream to play in the World Cup and Ronaldo has already done it three times with Portugal, displaying his dazzling skills to TV audiences right around the world. The Madrid magician was born to play in football's most famous event.

It was Ronaldo's seven goals in qualifying that booked Portugal's place in the 2006 World Cup. They were unbeaten on their way to the Finals and went on to win Group D as Ronaldo scored from the spot in the 2–0 victory over Iran.

Inspired by Ronaldo's attacking play, everyone was talking about Portugal as potential World Cup winners, and when they beat Holland 1–0 in the Last 16, there was real hope that the team could go all the way.

England stood in their way in the quarter-finals, but the match was scoreless so a penalty shootout beckoned. It fell to Ronaldo to take the all-important final kick and he kept his cool superbly to send keeper Paul Robinson the wrong way and win the match.

But although the semi-final against France brought heartbreak, as Zinedine Zidane scored the only goal of the game to knock Portugal out, Ronaldo and his nation's performances were recognised when they were given the FIFA award for the Most Entertaining Team.

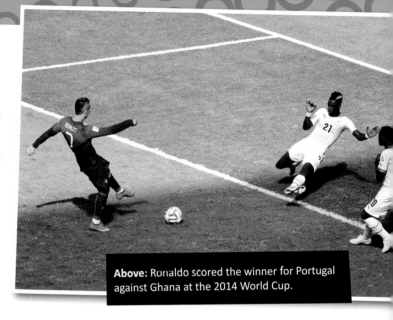

Above: Ronaldo scored the winner for Portugal against Ghana at the 2014 World Cup.

In 2008, Ronaldo was made Portugal captain at the age of just 23, only two months before the start of qualifying for the 2010 World Cup in South Africa. He rose to the challenge brilliantly and steered his team safely to the Finals.

Portugal were drawn in a tough group that had both Brazil and the Ivory Coast in it, but Ronaldo made sure they reached the knockout stages, scoring Portugal's seventh and final goal in their 7–0 demolition of North Korea in Cape Town. European champions Spain were the opposition in the last 16, but despite trying his luck with two trademark free-kicks, Ronaldo could not stop Portugal losing 1–0.

Portugal were back in World Cup action in 2014 thanks to four Ronaldo goals in qualifying and four more that destroyed Sweden in the play-offs, but despite his 50th international goal in the group game against Ghana, the Portuguese narrowly missed out on qualification for the knockout phase on goal difference.

Left: Ronaldo celebrates after helping Portugal to knock out England in the 2006 FIFA World Cup quarter-final.

Below: Ronaldo dances past Brazilian defender Juan during the goalless draw in the group stage of the 2010 FIFA World Cup in South Africa.

GREAT MANCHESTER UNITED GOALS

Ronaldo hit an incredible 118 goals in England in just 292 appearances for the mighty Manchester United. These are five of his very best…

MANCHESTER UNITED 2 *PORTSMOUTH 0*
PREMIER LEAGUE, JANUARY 30, 2008

Ronaldo is the most deadly player in the world with a long-range free-kick and this sensational 30-yard effort at Old Trafford was one of his very best. It flew like a laser-guided missile past Portsmouth keeper David James and into the top right corner of the net.

MANCHESTER UNITED 4 *ASTON VILLA 0*
PREMIER LEAGUE, MARCH 29, 2008

A beautiful goal that few other players could have dreamed of scoring, Ronaldo pounced on a loose ball in the penalty area and then cheekily back-heeled the ball behind his left leg, through a crowd of confused defenders and into the back of the net.

CHELSEA 1 MANCHESTER UNITED 1
CHAMPIONS LEAGUE, MAY 21, 2008

The best players always save their best for the very biggest matches and Ronaldo did the business in the UEFA Champions League Final in Moscow when he rose above the Chelsea defence to punch home Wes Brown's cross with a thumping header. United went on to win the trophy after a penalty-shootout.

Above: Ronaldo blasts the ball towards goal to give Manchester United a 1–0 win over FC Porto in the UEFA Champions League quarter-final.

Above: Rising high above the watching Chelsea defence, Ronaldo heads Manchester United's goal in the 2008 UEFA Champions League Final.

PORTO 0 **MANCHESTER UNITED 1**
CHAMPIONS LEAGUE, APRIL 15, 2009

United need to win to reach the semi-finals of the Champions League and Ronaldo delivered when it mattered most with a truly spectacular winner, a thunderbolt from 40 yards out that almost burst the net as it screamed past the stunned Porto keeper. Even Ronaldo's team-mates could not believe what they had just seen.

ARSENAL 1 **MANCHESTER UNITED 3**
CHAMPIONS LEAGUE, MAY 5, 2009

Another utterly unstoppable free-kick, Ronaldo unleashed this magnificent effort against Arsenal in the Champions League semi-final, blasting home from a wide angle past the wall and beating Gunners' keeper Manuel Almunia for pace and power at his near post.

MANCHESTER UNITED MILESTONES

Above: Ronaldo shows off the FA Cup after he had scored the opening goal of the 2004 final against Millwall, a match United won 3–0.

AUGUST 16, 2003
Ronaldo makes his debut for Manchester United, coming off the bench to replace Nicky Butt after 61 minutes in a 4–0 demolition of Bolton Wanderers at Old Trafford.

MAY 22, 2004
Scores the opening goal in a 3–0 win over Millwall in the FA Cup Final to lift his first piece of silverware with the Red Devils. He went on to win three Premier League titles (2006–07, 2007–08, 2008–09), two League Cups (2006 and 2009), the Champions League (2008) and the FIFA Club World Cup (2008) with United.

AUGUST 9, 2005
Scores the third goal in a 3–0 victory for United in their UEFA Champions League qualifier against Hungarian side Debrecen, his first-ever goal in Europe.

APRIL 1, 2007
Ronaldo is named the Football Writers' Association Footballer of the Year. He had already been voted the PFA Young Player, Players' Player and Fans' Player of the Year and became the first footballer ever to hold all four awards at the same time.

MARCH 19, 2008
Captains Manchester United for the first time in his career at the age of 23, scoring both of the goals in the Red Devils' comfortable 2-0 victory against Bolton Wanderers at Old Trafford.

NOVEMBER 15, 2008
Scores his 100th United goal in a 5–0 thrashing of Stoke City.

MAY 11, 2008
Scores in a 2–0 victory away at Wigan. It's his 31st Premier League goal of the season, a feat which earned him the European Golden Shoe award.

DECEMBER 2, 2008
Ronaldo collects the Ballon D'Or for the first time, the award given to the best footballer in Europe, beating Lionel Messi into second place in the vote.

JANUARY 12, 2009
Ronaldo becomes the first Premier League player ever to be voted FIFA World Player of the Year.

MAY 10, 2009
Scores in a 2–0 defeat of Manchester City at Old Trafford, his 118th and final goal for United in 292 appearances for the club.

DECEMBER 22, 2009
Collects the first-ever FIFA Puskas Award for the best goal of the year, his 40-yard thunderbolt against FC Porto in the UEFA Champions League.

REAL MADRID MILESTONES

Above: Ronaldo celebrates after scoring one of his five goals in the 9–1 victory over Grenada in La Liga on April 5, 2015.

JULY 1, 2009
Joins Real Madrid from Manchester United for world-record fee of £80 million.

APRIL 20, 2011
Scores the winner in extra-time of the Copa del Rey Final against Barcelona to lift his first trophy as a Madrid player.

MAY 21, 2011
Scores twice in an 8–1 demolition of Almeira in the final league game of the season. His double strike takes his tally for the season to 40, the first player in La Liga history to reach this number.

MAY 2, 2012
The striker finds the back of the net in a 3–0 away win against Athletic Bilbao, a result which gives Real Madrid the Spanish league title for a record-breaking 32nd time. He wins the La Liga player of the season.

MAY 13, 2012
Scores in a 4–1 league victory against Real Mallorca, a goal which makes Ronaldo the first player in the history of La Liga to score against every other team in the division in a single season.

MAY 8, 2013
Scores 200th goal for the club, against Malaga, to reach a double-century of strikes quicker than any of the other great players in the history of the club.

JANUARY 13, 2014
Ronaldo picks up the FIFA Ballon D'Or award for the world's best footballer for the second time.

MAY 24, 2014
Ronaldo scores in the 4–1 win over Atletico Madrid in the UFEA Champions League final. His 17th goal in 11 appearances breaks the previous Champions League/European Cup single-season record of 14.

Above: Ronaldo became Real's record goal scorer in October 2015 to cement his status as a Bernabeu legend.

AUGUST 12, 2014
Scores twice in Real Madrid's 2–0 victory over Sevilla in the UEFA Super Cup.

AUGUST 28, 2014
Wins UEFA Best Player in Europe award.

JANUARY 14, 2015
Wins the Ballon d'Or for the third time.

MARCH 10, 2015
Scores two goals in Real's 3–4 home defeat to Schalke in the Champions League to become the outright top scorer in all UEFA competitions (with 78 goals) and joins Lionel Messi as the Champions League's all-time top scorer.

APRIL 5, 2015
Scores five goals in one game for first time in professional career (including a nine-minute hat-trick) in a 9–1 victory over Granada in La Liga.

MAY 2, 2015
Scores 29th hat-trick of Real Madrid – against Sevilla – to break Alberto di Stefano's club record.

SEPTEMBER 12, 2015
Scores five goals in a game for the second time, in a 6–0 demolition of Espanyol, taking him to 230 league goals in 203 games and past Raúl's previous club record of 228.

OCTOBER 17, 2015
Becomes Madrid's all-time leading scorer in all competitions, with 324 goals, when he nets against Levante at thc Bernabeu.

APRIL 2, 2016
Nets a hat-trick in the Champions League semi-final second leg against Wolfsburg. His treble makes him the tournament's top scorer for the fourth consecutive season.

MAY 28, 2016
Converts the decisive penalty in the Champions League final shoot-out against Atletico Madrid as Real Madrid win the Cup for the 11th time.

AT HOME WITH RONALDO

When he's not showing off his unbelievable skills on the pitch, Ronaldo enjoys a quiet life away from the spotlight.

It's not easy being one of the most famous people on the planet and Ronaldo gets away from the pressures of playing for Real Madrid by spending his free time with family and friends. He became a father in July 2010 when Cristiano Ronaldo Junior was born and the star insists there is nowhere he would rather be than at home with his son.

"I am a very private person and I am down-to-earth," he said. "My family comes first – my son is the most important thing in my life. I salute him in the crowd every time I score a goal. After that it's the football that matters most to me. Money comes after that."

One thing that has always marked out Cristiano as a special player is his absolute dedication to football. He would much rather stay at home, looking after himself, than go out with his Bernabeu team-mates.

"Half the boys like to go to the disco. They like to party hard, they like to try to impress girls with champagne. But it's better to train hard and do well."

Ronaldo's father sadly died in 2005 but he remains very close to his mother, his sisters and his brother and despite all the money he earns, he is not that interested in cash.

"I bought my mother a £400,000 house in Portugal," he said. "She lives there with her partner and my son. I bought my sisters houses as well. My brother runs my nightclubs and various bars. I also own a hotel. But money hasn't changed me – I'm still the same person. I have my circle of friends, my club. People who've been with me a long time. I look after these people."

Ronaldo's fans got a rare glimpse inside his £5 million pad, just outside Madrid, in 2016 when he let in a camera crew and it made for fascinating viewing as we got to see how the star lives away from the spotlight.

There was of course a football pitch in his back garden but more surprising were a leopard skin duvet cover, statue of Buddha and, because it was December, Nativity scene set up by his private swimming pool.

One room is for all his trophies and winners' medals, but Ronaldo revealed the most important room in the house was his bedroom.

"I spend nearly half a day here," he said. "Because to perform good and be at a good level you have to rest good."

Below: Despite his massive fame and fortune, Ronaldo has always remained incredibly close to his mother Maria.

"*I always had a gift. I was shown the skills and I am a fantastic footballer but I do believe God gave me the gift.*"

Below: Ronaldo poses with his son beneath a statue of himself during the unveiling ceremony in his hometown in Funchal in December 2014.

Above: The Portuguese legend shows off the 2014 FIFA Ballon d'Or trophy he has just received. He is accompanied by his young son Cristiano, with whom he spends as much time as possible.

EUROPEAN CHAMPION

Ronaldo made his European Championship finals debut in 2004 and, 12 years later, he captained Portugal to glory in Euro 2016 in France.

Ronaldo first played for his country in August 2003, when he came off the bench against Kazakhstan. His Manchester United debut had come only four days before, against Bolton Wanderers, and was the start of an exciting new phase of his incredible career.

Less than a year later he was playing in Euro 2004, which was held in Portugal, and, although he was still only a teenager, Ronaldo was in amazing form as the hosts went all the way to the Final.

His goal in the semi-final win over Holland was crucial and despite Portugal losing in the Final to Greece, Ronaldo was named in the UEFA All-Star Team of the competition alongside star names like Zinedine Zidane, Frank Lampard, Michael Ballack and fellow Portuguese Luis Figo.

Above: Ronaldo celebrates after scoring against the Czech Republic in the 2008 European Championship finals.

Ronaldo scored an incredible seven goals in the qualifying matches as Portugal reached Euro 2008 in Switzerland and Austria. For the first time, he was handed the number seven shirt for a big tournament by manager Luiz Felipe Scolari.

A goal and a man-of-the-match performance in a 3–1 group stage win over the Czech Republic sent Portugal into the knockout phase, but Ronaldo could not stop Germany winning the quarter-final tie.

Ronaldo's third appearance in the European Championships came in 2012 in Poland and Ukraine and Portugal went into their final group game against Holland needing a win to stay in the tournament. Step forward Ronaldo with two goals to save the day.

Left: Ronaldo's first major tournament for Portugal was Euro 2004.

He was on target again with the only goal of the game against the Czech Republic in the quarter-finals. But there was heartbreak in the semi-final against Spain as Portugal lost on penalties. However, Ronaldo had shown his superstar status and was again named in the UEFA Team of the Tournament.

Ronaldo's greatest moment, however, came in 2016 as Portugal won their first major trophy after beating hosts France in the final in Paris in extra-time. Although he played in all seven games at Euro 2016, a bad knee injury sadly forced him off early in the final. An extra-time goal from Éder meant Ronaldo had finally won the trophy he'd always dreamed of.

"I'm so happy," he said. "This is something I have wanted for a long time now, ever since 2004. The Portuguese people deserve this; our players deserve this. This is one of the happiest moments of my career. I've always said I wanted to win a trophy with the national team and make history."

Below: Ronaldo scored three goals to help Portugal become European champions for the first time.

GREAT REAL MADRID GOALS

The Portuguese has been deadly in front of goal since he signed for Real Madrid in 2009 and here are five of his most spectacular efforts...

VILLAREAL 0 **REAL MADRID 2**
LA LIGA, SEPTEMBER 23, 2009

Ronaldo's blistering pace was incredible as he spun away from a desperate Villareal tackle on the halfway line and raced towards goal. His speed took him past another attempted tackle before he fired home into the bottom right corner.

REAL MADRID 6 VILLAREAL 2
LA LIGA, FEBRUARY 21, 2010

Even with his reputation for amazing free-kicks, few expected the Portuguese star to score against Villareal as he carefully placed the ball 35 yards out from goal. But he, of course had other ideas, launching a dazzling drive from the left that sailed beautifully into the top right corner.

RAYO VALLECANO 0 **REAL MADRID 1**
LA LIGA, FEBRUARY 26, 2012

A wonder goal worthy of winning any game, there seemed no danger when Rayo cleared a Real corner and Ronaldo was forced to retreat away from goal with the ball. Cue an outrageous, deadly back-heel that completely surprised the Vallecano defenders and keeper.

Above: Ronaldo is congratulated by Marcelo after his brilliant goal at Villareal's Madrigal in September 2009.

Right: Ronaldo's amazing back-heel against Rayo Vallecano in 2012 was simply world class.

REAL MADRID 2 BARCELONA 1
SPANISH SUPER CUP, AUGUST 29, 2012

The highlight of this remarkable goal was the amazing back-heel flick in the middle of the pitch over Gerard Pique that left the Barcelona defender stranded before Ronaldo smashed an unstoppable drive past Victor Valdes to win the Spanish Super Cup.

BORUSSIA DORTMUND 2 REAL MADRID 2
CHAMPIONS LEAGUE, SEPTEMBER 27, 2016

This stunning team goal featured all of Madrid's attacking stars and was finished off in style by Ronaldo. Gareth Bale's trademark burst from into the box was followed by a cheeky back-heel to slice open the Dortmund defence and there was Ronaldo, in the right place at the right time, to smash the ball into the bottom corner.

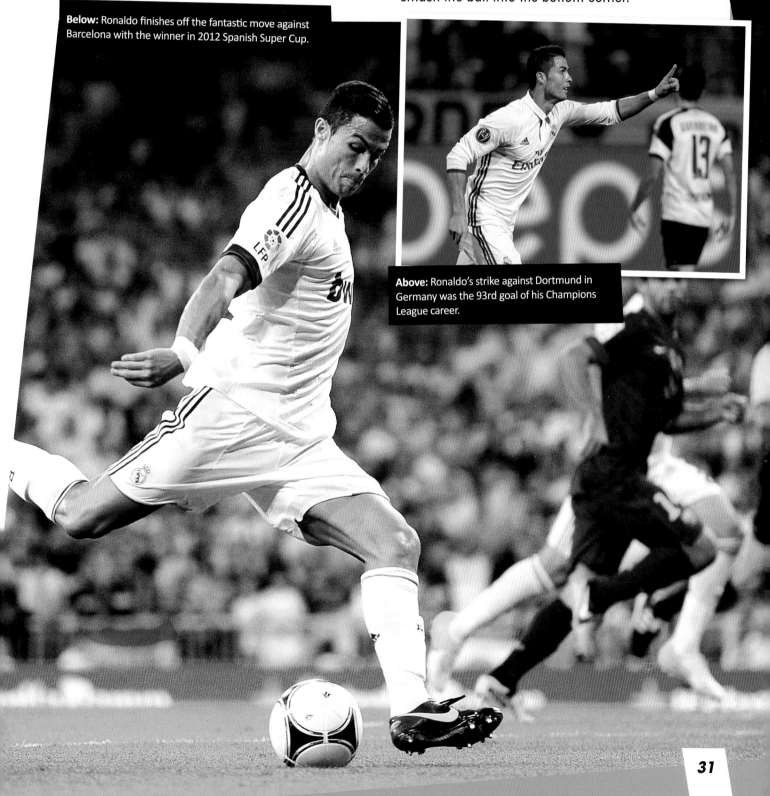

Below: Ronaldo finishes off the fantastic move against Barcelona with the winner in 2012 Spanish Super Cup.

Above: Ronaldo's strike against Dortmund in Germany was the 93rd goal of his Champions League career.

SUPER SKILLS

Ronaldo's amazing array of tricks and awesome talents
are what makes him the world's greatest player

IN THE AIR

Loads of Ronaldo's goals come from headers
and there are few players who can jump as
high or hang in the air as long before he
thumps home another headed effort. The
power he is able to generate with his snap
headers is awesome.

FABULOUS FLIP FLAP

One of the most outrageous
tricks in his box, Ronaldo's
"Flip Flap" gives defenders
sleepless nights. First he
moves the ball away with
the outside of his boot and
when the defender makes
his move, he rolls his studs
over the ball and in the
blink of an eye shifts it back
with his instep and away
from the tackle.

NEED FOR SPEED

Ronaldo is blessed with incredible speed and his
ability to race past players anywhere on the field is
one of the big reasons he is such a handful. Only
the very quickest defenders can live with him.

SUPERB SHOOTING

His long-range shooting is so good that every time he gets past the halfway line, the alarm bells start ringing for defenders. Ronaldo can hit a devastating range of shots, from the inswinger and the flat drive to the outswinger and the dipper.

FANTASTIC FREE-KICKS

Ronaldo has rewritten the rule book when it comes to free-kicks and there's almost no distance from which he can't go for goal. No one can get as much dip and swerve on the ball as the Portuguese but he also has the raw power needed to blast it past the keeper.

DAZZLING DRIBBLING

Speed alone is not enough to make a world-class player and it is Ronaldo's incredible dribbling at full speed that sets him apart. He bamboozles defenders with his unbelievable balance and ability to keep the ball just inches away from his feet.

THE STEP-OVER

Real Madrid fans have lost count of the number of confused defenders Ronaldo has beaten with his devastating step-over, sending defenders first one way and then the other before racing past them as they desperately try not to fall over.

WINNING CHAMPIONSHIPS

Ronaldo has been a key part of every team he has played in both in England and Spain. So he knows all about getting his hands on the most important trophies.

Only the most talented teams get to become league champions and Ronaldo has been the star in four of these sides, winning the Premier League three times in a row with Manchester United and La Liga with Real Madrid.

His first Premier League triumph came in the 2006–07 season. United hadn't won the championship for three years but Ronaldo was determined to put that right and after scoring on the opening day in a 5–1 demolition of Fulham at Old Trafford, there was no stopping him.

He finished the campaign as the Red Devils' top scorer with 17 league goals and Sir Alex Ferguson's side were champions again.

Ronaldo was even more deadly in 2007–08 as United defended their title. It was a close race with Chelsea all the way through the season, but his two priceless goals in a 4–1 defeat of West Ham United and another in a 2–0 victory away against Wigan Athletic in the last two games were enough to see off the Londoners' challenge.

United made it a magnificent hat-trick of titles in 2008–09 and once again Ronaldo was the difference as he again finished top scorer for the club with 18 great goals, more than a quarter of the team's Premier League total. He was definitely now an Old Trafford legend.

Real Madrid were desperate for Ronaldo to bring some of that magic to the Bernabeu after his record £80 million transfer in the summer of 2009 and he delivered just that in the 2011–12 season.

Barcelona had won three La Liga titles in a row but Ronaldo almost single-handedly brought that run to an end with a record-breaking season that saw Real Madrid crowned champions, nine points ahead of their big rivals.

The striker scored an unbelievable 46 times in 38 games – more than a third of Real Madrid's total of 121 La Liga goals.

Since claiming that 2011–12 title, Real have been runners-up three times (third once), and Ronaldo himself has twice finished as La Liga's top scorer (in 2013–14 and 2014–15), but he's still waiting for that second championship.

Right: Ronaldo's 46 goals in 38 La Liga games in 2011–12 saw Real Madrid crowned champions of Spain.

PORTUGAL MILESTONES

AUGUST 20, 2003
Makes debut for Portugal, aged just 18 years and seven months, against Kazakhstan.

JUNE 12, 2004
Scores in Portugal's 2–1 group stage defeat against Greece in Porto, his first international goal.

AUGUST 15, 2004
Scores for Portugal in a 2–1 group stage win over Morocco at the Athens Olympic Games.

JUNE 17, 2006
Ronaldo is on target from the penalty spot in a 2–0 victory over Iran in Frankfurt, his first World Cup Finals goal.

FEBRUARY 6, 2007
Captains Portugal for the first time as the team beat Brazil 2–0 in a friendly at the Emirates Stadium. When Carlos Queiroz is appointed coach in July 2008 Ronaldo becomes the permanent captain.

OCTOBER 16, 2012
By playing against Northern Ireland in a World Cup qualifier in Porto, Ronaldo joins Luis Figo and Fernando Couto as the only Portuguese players to win 100 caps.

NOVEMBER 19, 2013
A hat-trick from the Real Madrid star in the second leg of their play-off against Sweden sends Portugal to the 2014 World Cup. The goals take Ronaldo's total for Portugal in 2013 to 10, the best international haul of his career so far.

MARCH 5, 2014
The striker scores twice in a 5–1 friendly victory against Cameroon. It takes him to a total of 49 international goals and makes him Portugal's all-time leading scorer, breaking Pauleta's previous record of 47.

JUNE 26, 2014
The striker scores the winner in the group stage match against Ghana in the 2014 FIFA World Cup in Brazil, the 50th goal of his remarkable international career.

JUNE 18, 2016
Makes his 128th international appearance against Austria in Paris to become Portugal's most-capped player.

JULY 6, 2016
His goal against Wales in the Euro 2016 semi-final, sees Ronaldo match Michel Platini's record of nine in the European Championship finals.

OCTOBER 7, 2016
Ronaldo scores four goals in one international game for the first time as Portugal hammer Andorra 6–0 in a World Cup qualifier.

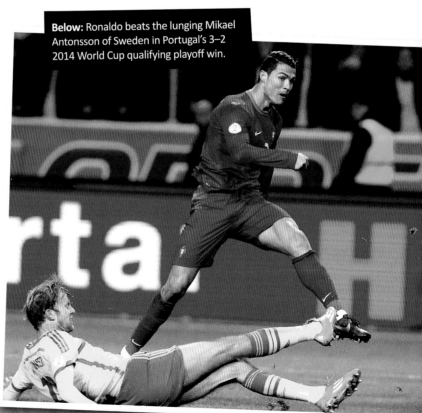

Below: Ronaldo beats the lunging Mikael Antonsson of Sweden in Portugal's 3–2 2014 World Cup qualifying playoff win.

Above: Ronaldo overtook Luis Figo's record of 127 Portugal caps against Austria at Euro 2016.

RONALDO IN NUMBERS

Cristiano Ronaldo breaks football records with a regularity that would impress a Swiss clock-maker. Here are some key numbers in the career of the man known as CR7.

Below: Ronaldo has been deadly in front of goal ever since he signed for Madrid.

9
The number of minutes it took the striker to smash three goals past Granada in April 2015, the fastest hat-trick in Real Madrid history.

244
The incredible number of fans, in millions, who were following Ronaldo on Facebook, Instagram and Twitter by October 2016.

133
Ronaldo's total number of caps for Portugal after playing in the Euro 2016 final against France.

548
His amazing tally of goals for club and country by the end of the 2015–16 season.

260
The total number of La Liga goals he had scored for Real Madrid in 236 appearances by the end of the 2015–16 season.

9

The number of times of Ronaldo has been named in the prestigious FIFA FIFPro World XI

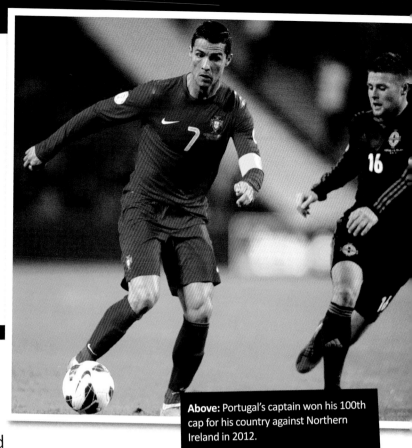

Above: Portugal's captain won his 100th cap for his country against Northern Ireland in 2012.

2021

The year in which Ronaldo's renewed contract with Real Madrid will come to an end.

37.66

Percentage of the total vote Ronaldo received to win the FIFA Ballon D'Or in 2014.

17

Ronaldo's goals total in the 2013–14 Champions League, a single-season record.

28

The shirt number (which he had worn for Sporting Lisbon) Ronaldo asked for when he signed for Manchester United in 2003. Sir Alex Ferguson refused and told him he would play in the famous number seven.

37

Number of Real Madrid hat-tricks claimed by Ronaldo by the end of 2015–16 – breaking Alfredo di Stefano's long-standing club record.

3

The number of times Ronaldo has won the prestigious Ballon d'Or award, given to the world's best player.

51

Goals total for Real in 2015–16, the sixth straight season he has passed 50 in all competitions.

1

According to ESPN in 2016, his ranking in the list of the world's most famous athletes.

TRAINING WITH RONALDO

The Real Madrid star may be blessed with incredible natural talent but he knows that means nothing unless he keeps working hard on the training ground.

Ronaldo was a skinny kid when he arrived at Old Trafford in 2003. The club had just spent £12.24 million on the teenager and although Sir Alex Ferguson and his coaching staff knew he had the skills to become a star, there were question marks about whether he was strong enough to cope with tough English football.

So Ronaldo hit the gym and over the next few seasons spent hours turning himself into a muscular and powerful player. The results were incredible and prove just how seriously he has always taken his training.

But it was not just building muscles that made Ronaldo such a hit at Manchester United. As well as getting stronger, the youngster would spend his spare time watching video clips of football legends like Pele and Johan Cruyff, studying their tricks and techniques so he could make his own game better.

"I am not a perfectionist but I like to feel that things are done well," he once said. "More important than that, I feel an endless need to learn, to improve, to evolve, not only to please the coach and the fans, but also to feel satisfied with myself. It is my conviction that there are no limits to learning, and that it can never stop, no matter what our age."

The striker took his great attitude with him when he signed for Real Madrid and he is famous for staying behind after training sessions to

Above: Practice makes perfect as Ronaldo works on his headers.

Right: Ronaldo warms up with his team-mates ahead of another Real Madrid training session.

practise his trademark free-kicks, constantly working on adding more swerve, dip and power to his shots.

Ronaldo also works very hard in training on his finishing. He will repeat one technique such as a near-post volley or back-post header four times before switching to another way of scoring. It's a way of practising that he learned at Old Trafford and ensures he's always ready when a goal-scoring chance comes along in a match.

"I am not a perfectionist but I like to feel that things are done well... More important than that, I feel an endless need to learn, to improve, to evolve, not only to please the coach and the fans, but also to feel satisfied with myself. It is my conviction that there are no limits to learning, and that it can never stop, no matter what our age."

Above: One of the greatest athletes in the game, Ronaldo is always working to get himself in perfect physical condition.

RONALDO'S SUPERSTAR TEAM-MATES

Although he's the main man at Real Madrid, Ronaldo is surrounded by world-class players at the Bernabeu.

GARETH BALE

Signed from Premier League side Tottenham Hotspur for a world record £85 million in the summer of 2013, the Welsh winger is an amazing natural talent who terrifies defenders with his pace, dribbling ability and eye for goal. Bale's lethal left foot compliments the right-footed Ronaldo beautifully. The deadly duo are capable of ripping apart even the meanest defences in La Liga and Europe.

SERGIO RAMOS

The Spain defender has been part of the Madrid first team since the start of the 2005–06 season and while Ronaldo is scoring goals at one end, it is Ramos's job to stop them at the other. Capped more than 100 times by Spain, Ramos can play at both full-back and in central defence and has won three La Liga titles with the club. Fast, strong and a great reader of the game, he is one of the toughest defenders in world football.

LUKA MODRIC

If Ronaldo is the man who provides the fireworks at the Bernabeu, it is Modric who makes the Madrid midfield tick. Signed from Tottenham Hostpur for £30 million in August 2012, the Croatian maestro initially struggled to find a place in the team under Jose Mourinho, but flourished under the managerial reign of Carlo Ancelotti. His ability to find the perfect pass for Real's frontmen was evident during Real's march to the Champions League crown in 2014.

TONI KROOS

A World Cup winner in Brazil in 2014, Kroos completed his move to Madrid just four days after Germany had beaten Argentina in the final. A hardworking but creative midfielder at Bayern Munich, he won three league titles and the Champions League before heading to Spain. He missed just eight of 72 La Liga matches in his first two seasons in Madrid and started in the 2016 Champions League final when Real beat Atletico Madrid.

RONALDO AND HIS FANS

One of the most popular players on the planet, Ronaldo is worshipped by millions of supporters all over the world.

If you want an idea just how much Real Madrid supporters love their Portuguese superstar, you only need to watch a video of Ronaldo's official unveiling to the fans in 2009. Eighty thousand people packed into the club's Bernabeu stadium to welcome him to Spain.

Most top European clubs don't even get that many supporters for a match, but Ronaldo was so popular in Madrid that there wasn't a spare seat in the ground when he arrived in Spain – before he had even kicked a ball!

The supporters rushed to buy Real Madrid shirts with Ronaldo's name and number nine on the back (since 2010 he has worn the number seven) and just nine months later the club had sold an unbelievable 1.2 million shirts in Madrid alone. That equalled over £80 million worth of sales, more than it cost the club to sign the player from Manchester United!

By the end of 2014, Ronaldo shirts were the best-selling replica shirts in the world, beating Barcelona's Lionel Messi into second place.

There are hundreds of unofficial Ronaldo fan clubs around the world and he is one of the most followed people on social media. An astonishing 240 million

Above: The Madrid superstar is a heartthrob as well as a football hero.

fans worldwide were following his official Facebook, Instagram and Twitter accounts by summer 2016.

Ronaldo has repaid his fans many times for their support. In January 2014 he invited a young Real Madrid supporter suffering from cancer to watch a game at the Bernabeu in his own VIP box and in March he agreed to pay £70,000 for another young fan to

Right: Ronaldo's popularity is shown by the millions of replica shirts that have been sold across the globe.

RAUL 7

KAKA 8

RONALDO 9

LASS

BENZEM 11

44

S/M

undergo life-saving brain surgery. In February 2016 the Madrid hero celebrated his 31st birthday and to mark his special day he posted a video message to his fans on his Twitter account. "I wanted to thank you for the messages you have sent me," he said. "As you know it's my birthday. Thirty-one years old. So thank you all! We're together. And please keep on supporting me like you do."

Above: Ronaldo makes a Portugal fan's dreams come true by handing him his game shirt after the Euro 2008 match against the Czech Republic.

GREAT PORTUGAL GOALS

The all-time leading scorer for his country, Ronaldo has hit some unbelievable wonder goals while on international duty for his beloved Portugal.

PORTUGAL 7 *RUSSIA 1*

WORLD CUP QUALIFIER, OCTOBER 13, 2004

There was a stunned silence inside the stadium in Lisbon when Ronaldo scored this wonder goal. He collected the ball just inside enemy territory and, when faced with five Russian defenders, blasted a fierce, dipping drive from outside the area into the top corner.

DENMARK 2 *PORTUGAL 1*

EURO 2012 QUALIFIER, OCTOBER 11, 2011

His greatest free-kick for his country, this 40-yard effort had everything – power, swerve and dramatic dip at the end. The ball flew just under the crossbar and into the net.

NETHERLANDS 1 *PORTUGAL 2*

EURO 2012 GROUP B, JUNE 17, 2012

Ronaldo's two goals fired Portugal into the quarter-finals and his second was a work of art. Collecting a pass from Nani, he dummied a shot that left Dutch defender Gregory van der Wiel on his backside before driving low into the net.

Below: Pauleta leaps on Ronaldo's shoulders after another goal in the 2004 rout of Russia.

Above: Dutch goalkeeper Maarten Stekelenburg is helpless as Ronaldo scores one of his two goals to help Portugal reach the Euro 2012 quarter-finals.

SWEDEN 2 **PORTUGAL 3**

WORLD CUP PLAY-OFF, NOVEMBER 19, 2013

One of Ronaldo's greatest games for Portugal, his hat-trick booked the team's place in the World Cup Finals. His third goal was a belter as he glided into the Sweden penalty area, expertly took the ball past the goalkeeper and calmly stroked the ball home.

PORTUGAL 2 WALES 0

EURO 2016 SEMI-FINAL, JULY 6, 2016

The greatest players score when it really matters and Ronaldo did exactly that when he broke the deadlock in the 50th minute of the Euro 2016 semi-final against Wales in Lyon. Full-back Raphaël Guerreiro fired in an accurate, out-swinging cross from the left wing, Ronaldo jumped brilliantly above the Wales defence and powered home a superb header.

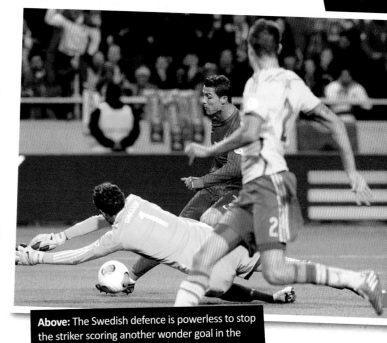

Above: The Swedish defence is powerless to stop the striker scoring another wonder goal in the 2014 World Cup qualifying playoff.

Below: Ronaldo's goal against Wales in Euro 2016 was the most important of his record-breaking international career.

47

WORLD TRAVELLER

Wherever he goes on the planet, Ronaldo is sure to make headlines and is always guaranteed a warm welcome from his fans.

It is a good job that Ronaldo is not a nervous flyer because the superstar has clocked up thousands of miles in the air since he flew to England to sign for Manchester United back in 2003. There are few countries that he has not yet visited as a Real Madrid player, Portugal captain, charity ambassador or holidaymaker.

Modern footballers travel huge distances to play games and Ronaldo has been as far afield as China with Real Madrid for pre-season tours before returning to Spain for La Liga action.

Real Madrid traditionally set up camp in the USA every summer to get the squad ready for the new season and it was in 2013 that Ronaldo caught up with David Beckham in Los Angeles, a meeting of two of the most famous players in the history of the game.

But it is not just football that sees Ronaldo reaching for his passport. The star represents a number of charities and in 2013 he made the journey to Indonesia in his role as an ambassador for the Mangrove Care Forum, an organisation that protects the natural environment in the country.

Below: (from left) Ronaldo, Iker Casillas and David Beckham during an airport stopover on Madrid's preseason tour to the United States.

In the same year he also visited a secondary school in Singapore to support the launch of a new scholarship scheme for talented young athletes.

His football and charity work means Ronaldo has a hectic schedule, but there is still time for holidays with his son, Cristiano Junior, and family. In recent years the striker has jetted off to Miami, Thailand and St Tropez to get away from it all.

He certainly deserved a break after inspiring Portugal's incredible victory at Euro 2016 and as soon as the tournament was over Ronaldo headed to a private yacht off Ibiza to relax. But he didn't get an all-over tan because he wore a brace on his left knee to help his recovery from the injury he suffered in the final!

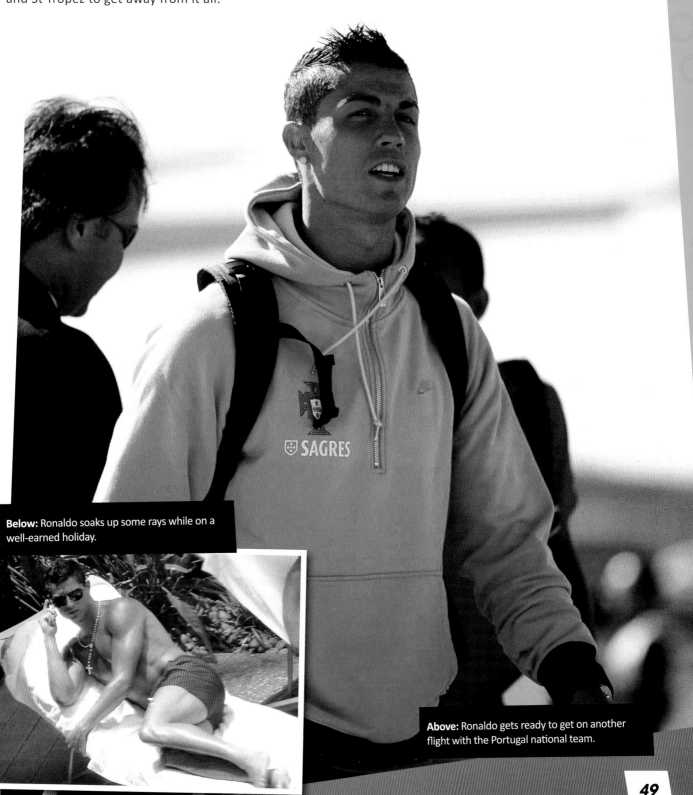

Below: Ronaldo soaks up some rays while on a well-earned holiday.

Above: Ronaldo gets ready to get on another flight with the Portugal national team.

EUROPEAN SUPERSTAR

The Champions League is the biggest club competition on the planet and Ronaldo has won it three times in his awesome career.

Cristiano Ronaldo made his Champions League debut for Manchester United against Stuttgart on October 10, 2003, and has gone on to enjoy a remarkable love affair with European football's premier club tournament.

His breakthrough season in the competition came in the 2007–08 season. United had lost in the semi-finals the previous year, but with Ronaldo in sensational form they made it all the way to the Final to face Chelsea in Moscow, the capital of Russia.

Ronaldo had already scored seven goals on the way to the big match and he was on target again in Russia with an unstoppable first-half header that set up a penalty shootout after extra-time. United held their nerve to be crowned European champions for a third time in the club's history. Ronaldo's haul of eight goals made him the tournament's top scorer.

The striker's next great Champions League season came in 2012–13, when he once again finished as top scorer. Ronaldo fired in an incredible 12 goals, including two in a 3–2 last-16 win over United, as Real Madrid made it to the semi-finals for a second year running.

Ronaldo's form in the 2013–14 tournament was even better. He scored nine goals in the group stages, including a hat-trick against Galatasaray, and seven more in the knockout phase as Madrid marched into the Final to face city rivals Atletico Madrid.

The Final in Lisbon saw Real taken into extra-time by Atletico, but Ronaldo was on target from the penalty spot to seal a famous 4–1 win and secure the second Champions League winner's medal of his amazing career. In total, the striker scored 17 goals in just 11 games – moving to second all-time on the Champions Legaue – as Real ruled Europe for a record 10th time.

Ten titles became a magnificent 11 in 2015–16 as Ronaldo and Real were crowned champions as they again beat Atletico in the final in Rome. The match finished 1–1 and went to a penalty shootout, when it was Ronaldo, naturally, who stepped up to take Real's winning spot-kick.

His 16 goals in the 2015–16 Champions League were again the best in the competition and it took him to a total of 93 all time, easily the most in the tournament's 61-year history.

Above: Manchester United's team photo before the 2008 Champions League final against Chelsea.

Below: Ronaldo's penalty in the 2016 final shoot-out ensured he collected his third Champions League winners' medal.

Above: Ronaldo, who scored in Real's 4–1 win over neighbours Atletico in 2014, shows off the Champions League trophy after becoming one of the few players to be a winner with two clubs.

RONALDO AND HIS COACHES

The world's greatest footballer has played for some of the game's finest managers during his record-breaking career.

SIR ALEX FERGUSON

The man who brought him to Manchester United in 2003, Ferguson was a massive influence on Ronaldo's early career. Ferguson was the man who first switched Ronaldo from the wing to striker. Ronaldo then helped the Red Devils win a hat-trick of Premier League titles and the Champions League.

"I HAVE NOTHING BUT PRAISE FOR THE BOY. HE IS EASILY THE BEST PLAYER IN THE WORLD. HIS CONTRIBUTION AS A GOAL THREAT IS UNBELIEVABLE. HIS STATS ARE INCREDIBLE. STRIKES AT GOAL, ATTEMPTS ON GOAL, RAIDS INTO THE PENALTY BOX, HEADERS. IT IS ALL THERE. ABSOLUTELY ASTOUNDING."

Sir Alex Ferguson

JOSE MOURINHO

The two Portuguese teamed up with spectacular results at Real Madrid between 2010 and 2013 and with the duo together at the Bernabeu, Madrid toppled Barcelona as La Liga champions. Mourinho's famous management skills got the very best out of Ronaldo.

"IF MESSI IS THE BEST ON THE PLANET, RONALDO IS THE BEST IN THE UNIVERSE."

Jose Mourinho

CARLO ANCELOTTI

Another manager at Madrid, the famous Italian has won the league title in Italy, England and France and Ronaldo grew even more under his leadership. Ancelotti gave the Portuguese star plenty of freedom to attack and Ronaldo responded with some amazing performances for Real.

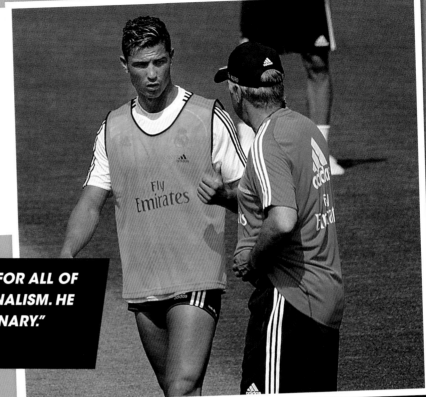

"RONALDO IS A UNIQUE PLAYER FOR ALL OF HIS TALENT AND HIS PROFESSIONALISM. HE IS A PLAYER WHO IS EXTRAORDINARY."
Carlo Ancelotti

ZINEDINE ZIDANE

A Real legend in his own right, the Frenchman became the Bernabeu boss in January 2016 after Rafa Benitez was sacked. Together with his star Portuguese player, he masterminded Real's Champions League triumph. An amazing entertainer in his own playing days, Zidane understands Ronaldo perfectly.

"WHAT CAN I SAY ABOUT CRISTIANO RONALDO? HE IS THE BEST PLAYER IN THE WORLD. HE IS A SPECIAL PLAYER."
Zinedine Zidane

GLOBAL SUPERSTAR

An ambassador for some of the world's biggest brands and the face of Pro Evolution Soccer, Ronaldo even has his own line of clothing and a museum dedicated to him.

Football is the most popular sport on the planet and it's no surprise that its greatest player is known all around the world. The striker may be a hero in his native Portugal, but he's just as famous in Peru, the Philippines and Poland.

"All around the world I have to deal with my fame," Ronaldo said. "I can't go anywhere without being recognised, which can be very hard."

His global reputation has seen the star sign lucrative sponsorship deals with Coca-Cola, men's fashion company Emporio Armani, Motorola and KFC and he has appeared in a series of TV adverts for sportswear giants Nike which have been broadcast all over the world.

In 2006 Ronaldo opened a fashion store called "CR7" (his trademarked initials and shirt number) on the island of Madeira and two years later he set up a second shop in the Portuguese capital Lisbon.

In December 2013 Ronaldo launched a museum, the "Museu CR7", in his hometown of Funchal to celebrate his amazing career. Thousands of fans from all over the world flocked to see the trophies, medals and memorabilia on show, underlining the strength of his global popularity.

The following month he was named the Grand Officer of the Order of Prince Henry by the Portuguese President, an exclusive honour that showed the impact Ronaldo has made in his own country.

The superstar was also honoured by the world famous Madame Tussauds in London when they unveiled a waxwork of him ahead of the 2010 FIFA World Cup. Ronaldo attended the opening ceremony in person with fellow footballers David Beckham, Pele and Steven Gerrard.

In 2014 the famous American magazine Time named Ronaldo among the 100 most influential people in the world while, in November 2015, a documentary film about his incredible life and career, called Ronaldo, was released in cinemas. After Portugal's dramatic win over France in the Euro 2016 final, Madeira Airport in Funchal, his hometown, was renamed Cristiano Ronaldo Airport in honour of his amazing performances in the tournament.

Right: Ronaldo greets the President of Portugal in Lisbon in 2014 when he received his country's equivalent of a knighthood.

Above: Ronaldo's statue at the museum dedicated to him in his native Funchal, Madeira – and it is the island's capital pictured in the background.

Above: Ronaldo is one of the highest paid athletes signed up by sportswear giants Nike.

RECORD BREAKER

Ronaldo has smashed countless records and reached many marvellous milestones for both club and country during his fabulous career.

Above: Ronaldo celebrates becoming Portugal's all-time leading goalscorer (with 49) after netting a double against Cameroon in March 2014.

Ronaldo has rewritten the record books since he signed for Real Madrid and he is now the fastest player in the club's history to reach the 50, 100, 150 and 200 league goal milestones. He is also the quickest player to reach 200 goals in La Liga history.

Ronaldo is the only man to have won, in a single season, all of: domestic League, Cup and Super Cup; UEFA Champions League and FIFA Club World Cup; domestic Golden Shoe and Player of the Year; plus Ballon d'Or – World Player of the Year – at two different clubs.

He is only the player to have scored in four European Championship finals (2004, 2008, 2012 and 2016).

The striker jointly holds the record for finding the back of the net in successive Champions League games, scoring in six games in a row for Real Madrid in the competition. His hot streak started with a 4–1 win over Ajax in December 2012 and after finding the back of the net home and away against both Manchester United and Galatasaray (to reach five games in a row), he made it six on the bounce with a goal in the first leg of the semi-final against Borussia Dortmund.

In 2015–16 he became the first man ever to grab three Champions League hat-tricks in one season.

Ronaldo has been named in UEFA's Team of the Year 10 times – more than any other player.

Unstoppable in front of goal for Madrid in 2011–12, he scored a club record 61 goals in all competitions.

The striker shares the record for the most goals scored in a 38-game Premier League season, hitting the back of the net 31 times in 2007–08. Alan Shearer, for Blackburn in 1995–96, and Luis Suarez, in 2013–14, also scored 31 goals.

The Portuguese set a new record as the first player ever to score in six successive "El Clasico" games between Real Madrid and Barcelona. His amazing run began in the Copa del Rey in January 2012 and carried on until the two teams met in La Liga in October. The remarkable run brought seven goals in six appearances.

Above: Ronaldo won the Ballon d'Or as a Manchester United player in 2008 and a Real Madrid one in 2013 and 2014.

WHAT NEXT FOR RONALDO?

He has already achieved so much in more than a decade as a professional footballer but the ambitious Ronaldo never gets tired of success.

Although he celebrated his 31st birthday in 2016, Ronaldo is fitter, stronger and even hungrier for success today than the teenager who first broke into the Sporting Lisbon team back in 2002. Nobody knows how many more records he will break and how many more trophies he will lift before he hangs up his boots.

His incredible form in recent seasons led to rumours of a possible move to another big European club, but Real Madrid moved quickly and, in November 2016, his fans were celebrating when it was announced he had signed a new contract to keep him at the Bernabeu until June 2021.

It means the Madrid fans can look forward to many more seasons watching Ronaldo's genius.

"I'm going to be here for another five years, but let it be known this will not be my last contract," he said after agreeing to the new deal.

"I have said many times that I carry this club in my heart, it is part of me and it is a special time in my life.

"Of course I would like to end my career at this club. I want to be here for many years to come. I want to continue rewriting history at this club."

The even better news for Madrid's supporters is their hero is already thinking beyond 2021 and admits he wants to keep terrifying La Liga defences for another 10 years.

"I'm going to retire at Real Madrid when I'm over 40," he said in an interview. "I'm very happy here and I work hard to achieve things. For me La Liga is the best league in the world. It's a privilege to be here. I want to stop playing at age 41 or something like that."

If Ronaldo is lucky with injury, it would be a brave man to bet against him making good on his promise.

Below: The striker is all smiles after winning his 100th cap for Portugal in 2012.

Right: The 2016 Champions League was the eighth trophy of Ronaldo's amazing Real Madrid career.

Cristiano Ronaldo

Above: Ronaldo and Real Madrid president Florentino Perez, the man who offered the superstar a new contract.

QUIZ TIME

Here are 20 questions to test just how much you know about Cristiano Ronaldo. All the answers can be found in the preceding pages of this book.

1. On which Portuguese island was Ronaldo born in 1985?
2. What did Ronaldo's mother Maria do for a living?
3. What was the name of the first amateur team he played for as an eight-year-old?
4. How many goals did Ronaldo score on his league debut for Sporting Lisbon?
5. What number shirt did he wear in his one season playing for Sporting Lisbon?
6. How much did Manchester United pay to sign Ronaldo from Sporting Lisbon in 2003?
7. Which player wore the number seven shirt at Old Trafford before Ronaldo joined the club?
8. Against which team did the player make his Champions League debut for United in October 2003?
9. In what year did the forward make his European Championship debut?
10. Against which country did Ronaldo score the winning penalty in the 2006 World Cup quarter-final?

Above: See question 5. Ronaldo made his name for Sporting Lisbon wearing which shirt number?

Above: See question 16. Ronaldo helps himself to hat-trick in 2010 but against which Spanish side?

11 Against which team did Ronaldo first captain Portugal in 2007?

12 How many goals did he score during the 2007–08 Premier League season when Manchester United were crowned champions?

13 Against which team did he score a 40-yard screamer in 2009 to win the first-ever FIFA Puskas Award for the best goal of the year?

14 Ronaldo holds the record for the most goals scored in a Champions League season. How many did he score in 2013–14?

15 What milestone did Ronaldo reach when he scored against Levante in October 2015?

16 How many times has the Portuguese finished the season as La Liga's top scorer?

17 Whose old record of 127 caps for Portugal did Ronaldo break in 2016?

18 How many goals did the striker score at Euro 2016 as Portugal were crowned champions?

19 How many times has the star been named in the FIFA FIFPro World XI?

20 Which team lost to Ronaldo and Real Madrid in the 2016 Champions League final?

ANSWERS – SEE PAGE 63

PICTURE QUIZ

Cristiano Ronaldo is no stranger to getting his hands on silverware but can you spot which trophies the star is holding in these pictures? The answers are on the opposite page.

1

2

3

4

5

6

CREDITS

The publishers would like to thank the following sources for their kind permission to reproduce the pictures in this book. The page numbers for each of the photographs are listed below, giving the page on which they appear in the book and any location indicator (T-top, B-bottom, C-centre, L-left, R-right).

Above: Ronaldo strikes the penalty which sealed Real Madrid's 4–1 victory over Atletico and the club's 10th UEFA Champions League in May 2014.

Getty Images: 49R; /Gonzalo Arroyo Moreno: 53T; /Matthew Ashton – AMA: 62TR; /Shaun Botterill: 50, 51BR; /Martin Bureau/AFP: 2; /Victor Carretero: 30L; /City Files/WireImage: 26; /Fabrice Coffrini/AFP: 27R, 57, 62BR; /Nuno Correia/Allsport: 10R; /Antonio Cotrim/AFP: 13; /Gregorio Cunha/AFP: 8TR, 27BL; /Helios de la Rubia: 24; /Gregg DeGuire/FilmMagic: 41, 48; /Adrian Dennis/AFP: 22L; /Denis Doyle: 9, 25, 30BR, 35, 42BR, 62TC; /Paul Ellis/AFP: 47B; /Don Emmert/AFP: 55R; /Franck Fife/ AFP: 6L, 22-23, 28BL, 63; /Charley Gallay/FilmMagic: 49BL; /Laurence Griffiths: 15, 51T; /Valery Hache/AFP: 4-5; /Matthias Hangst: 58BR; /Mike Hewitt: 62TL; /Karim Jaafar/AFP: 19; /Liu Jin/AFP: 44R; /Jose Jordan/AFP: 62BL; /Jasper Juinen: 33R, 40R, 44BR, 61; /Talar Kalajian/AFP: 40BR; /Andre Kosters/AFP: 14L, 54; /Jean-Pierre Ksiazek/AFP: 17; /Christopher Lee: 55L; /Bryn Lennon: 28R; /Francisco Leong/AFP: 29, 52TL; /Jochen Luebke/AFP: 18BL; /Pierre-Philippe Marcou/AFP: 6R, 59; /Angel Martinez: 3; /Jamie McDonald: 21, 46L; /Jonathan Nackstrand/AFP: 47T; /Thomas Niedermueller: 45; /Pedro Nunes/AFP: 56; /John Peters: 14R; /Dani Pozo/AFP: 32; /Cristina Quicler/AFP: 38; /David Ramos: 31B; /Jaime Reina/AFP: 42L, 52BR; /Miguel Riopa/AFP: 20, 39, 58R; /Clive Rose: 33TL; /Martin Rose: 36; /STR/AFP: 16L; /Evaristo Sa/AFP: 18TR; /Antonio Simoes/AFP: 16R, 60; /TF-Images: 31R; /Bob Thomas/Popperfoto: 37; /VI Images: 8BL, 10L, 11, 12, 43R, 53B; /Visionhaus/Corbis: 7, 43BL; /Ian Walton: 46R. **Shutterstock:** /Marco Iacobucci/EPP: 64

Every effort has been made to acknowledge correctly and contact the source and/or copyright holder of each picture and Carlton Books Limited apologises for any unintentional errors or omissions that will be corrected in future editions of this book.

ANSWERS

PICTURE QUIZ

1 Ronaldo with the Carling (Football League) Cup (2009). **2** Ronaldo with La Liga trophy (2012). **3** Ronaldo shows off the UEFA Champions League trophy (2016). **4** Ronaldo holding the Copa del Rey (2011). **5** Ronaldo lifting the FA Cup (2004). **6** Ronaldo with the FIFA Ballon d'Or (2015).

QUIZ TIME

1 Madeira. **2** Cook. **3** Andorinha. **4** Two. **5** 28. **6** £12.24 million. **7** David Beckham. **8** Stuttgart. **9** 2004. **10** England. **11** Brazil. **12** 31. **13** Porto. **14** 17. **15** He became Real's all-time top scorer with 324 goals. **16** Three. **17** Luis Figo. **18** Three. **19** Nine. **20** Atletico Madrid.